Shelving and Storage

Contents

WITHDRAWN FROM STOCK

Introduction

Having bits and pieces around us is one of the occupational hazards of being human. It's all very well trying to live a minimalist existence, but it is not very practical or realistic, or, for that matter, very interesting. Eventually, when the clutter of life begins to get on top of you, you can't find that particular tool or gadget, or you notice yourself tripping over Wellingtons and toys, then it is time to order your life.

Homes & Ideas: Shelving and Storage aims to give you lots of practical advice on finding original and attractive ways to stack, pack, hide, disguise, or even display, the important, though not always very pretty, essentials of life, whether it be the ironing board, the garden rake or your grandmother's Minton dinner service.

You will find ideas on making the most of space in your home (from the attic to the garden shed), ways to brighten up even the dullest cupboards and shelves (with detailed step-by-step instructions), and, most importantly, cheap but effective containers for hiding away oddments until they are needed.

There are guidelines on choosing the right materials for building shelving, with expert advice on the correct way to make sure the shelves are safely constructed and fixed in place, so that they will serve you for a lifetime.

Keeping your life in some kind of order when you are busy need not be difficult or expensive, and you will find plenty of cost-saving ideas for the conventional and the not-so-conventional solutions to your storage problems.

1 Making the most of space

Whether you are trying to create order out of existing chaos, or planning to move into a new house, the best starting point is a masterplan. Ask yourself what it is that you need to store, then list the items in groups. Some items, especially kitchen utensils, are in use all the time. Others see the light of day perhaps once a year – the stand for the Christmas tree, for example, or your best crystal glasses. The following list of items needing to be stored might get you thinking along the right lines:

- luggage
- coats, hats and umbrellas
- Christmas decorations
- sports and camping gear
- ladders
- cleaning equipment, mops and brooms
- ironing board
- DIY tools
- painting and decorating equipment
- records and CDs
- books
- vases
- bedding
- camp beds
- winter/summer clothing
- clothes/toys children have out-grown
- summer garden furniture in the winter
- garden implements and mowers
- barbecue and picnic basket

In the kitchen:
- china and glass
- cook books
- cans and jars
- extra large pans (fish kettles, preserving pans)
- napkins and table cloths

It is quite a list once you start. Now, rewrite you masterplan, putting everything in order of use and ease of access, making a note of what you use often (the secateurs, screwdrivers, a dictionary, the phone book), and less often (suitcases, an extension lead, the cool box). Then be brutal: could some things go to the charity shop or the dump? The chances are, if things have been in the back of the loft for years, are still in the removal boxes from your last house move, or are unrecognisable under a layer of dust, you probably don't need them anyway.

Now make a note of specific requirements: tools need to be kept dry and in a safe place away from children, and wine needs to be kept dark and cool. In July, your winter woollies need to be in clean storage, away from mice and moths. Everything needs to be easily accessible, for your own safety, even if you need to use a ladder.

Now you can work out exactly what needs to be put away, and where it might find a home.

Finding space

Take a good look at your surroundings, and think about how they might work best for you. Most people who live in a house have access to a loft. This is the ideal space for storing important but little used items, but do make sure that access is good. Integral ladders which pull down from the loft hatch are available from DIY stores and will dispense with the need to fetch a ladder from the garage every time you need to get down a suitcase. Safety within the loft is very important: ensure that you put down boards (also available from DIY stores) across the roofing timbers before you walk around in the loft and possibly put your foot through the ceiling of the room below.

Space beneath the stairs in a hallway is always adaptable for storing coats, hats and gloves, whether you decide to install a cupboard, or simple pegs with a chest of drawers for the accessories.

A dry, clean cellar is an added bonus, providing easy-to-reach storage space. There are safety precautions here too: make sure that the stairs down to the cellar are secure, with a handrail if they are steep. You may also need to ensure good ventilation if storing food.

Make the most of blank or awkward areas, which have no particular use but which could be adapted easily. The obvious example is the chimney breast with alcoves deep enough to accommodate shelves or cupboards. Even a disused fireplace could be filled with shelves or hung with cupboard doors.

Above: **Hallways and landings are ideal for storing books, which require only shallow shelving and fit well into a narrow space.**
Right: **The corner of this hallway has been put to good use for coats and outdoor shoes. A simple plywood or chipboard shelf is supported by shelving brackets, then hidden beneath fabric (the lower edge hemmed) which is attached to the skirting board using tacks. Curtain track is hung from the front of the shelf to support a curtain and attractive fixed pelmet. The result is not expensive, but very effective.**

Below: **Awkward space, under a stair, by a back door or in a cellar might be used to store wine. Wine racks are designed to be very adaptable so that they can be stacked in different shapes. Here, the white walls and tile floor will also keep the wine cool. The dark environment of an under-stairs cupboard, laid with a stone or tile floor, would work equally well (see Chapter 2 for ideas on storing wine in the right conditions).**

Above: **Many houses, especially older ones, have plenty of space under the eaves which can be put to good use. Here, dead space is made to work as a walk-in dressing room. The highest point of the ceiling is kept for standing room, and a clothes rail runs the full length of each side. The small spice drawers are perfect for storing accessories and smaller items of clothing.**

Opposite: **Attractive, but rarely used, baskets and a champagne bucket are cleverly kept out of the way in this small kitchen. A clothes airer would be just as good for hanging pans, colanders, dried flowers or baskets, attached with butchers' hooks which are available from most kitchen shops (see Chapter 3 for ideas on hanging utensils around a kitchen). A single shelf set above head height would provide additional storage space for any pans, tinned food, or bottles which are not often needed.**

DISNEY ANIMATIONS AND ANIMATORS   WHITNEY MUSEUM OF AMERICAN ART   24 JUNE–6 SEPTEMBER 1981

Look to the skies! The space above your head may be going to waste, when it could provide additional storage space. A single shelf running around the wall will prove useful and in a high-ceilinged room there may be enough space for several shelves or even cupboards. Make sure you can reach storage spaces safely using a stool or steps to avoid accidents.

Opposite: **The space above this bed (between the wardrobes) has been fitted with cupboards, where items used rarely can be kept well hidden. Out of season clothes, blankets and spare bedding would store well up here.**
Below: **The space above a fitted or free standing wardrobe can be somewhere to keep hats and accessories, packed away in pretty boxes which co-ordinate with the wall paper (see Chapter 4 for how to cover your own hat boxes).**

Making space work harder

If you have the luxury of bedroom space that is being under-used, fill it with spacious cupboards or wardrobes, fitting out one side with shelves and drawers, another with a hanging rail. Make use of the inside of wardrobe doors, on which you might hang small accessories: ties,

belts, necklaces. Storing things neatly and in an organised way makes them easier to find, and makes the best use of the space (see page 18 for space saving ideas). Disguising wardrobe fronts with mirrors is an old trick for making small spaces look larger.

Above: **One section of these Gothic-shaped wardrobes (which reflect the Victorian architecture of the house) has been turned into shelves to make a narrow space work harder.**

Right: **The bathroom is another room which needs plenty of storage space, though towels, jars and cosmetics need to be kept close at hand. The blank space under this basin provides four cupboards and two drawers, whilst leaving a useful sideboard around the basin itself. Cupboards might also be put around the bathroom mirror – any containing medicines must be lockable and out of the reach of small children. Avoid hanging the medicine cupboard above the lavatory, where it would be easy for a child to reach.**

Bottom: **When planning a new kitchen, make a list of everything you need to store, including food mixers and large serving plates which take up a great deal of room, so you can be sure it will all fit in. Kitchen designers have plenty of tricks for using up every bit of available space, from larder cupboards to drawers in the kickboard, so a wander round kitchen showrooms might give you some unexpected ideas. A clever technique is to utilise the blank side of a kitchen cupboard by installing narrow shelves, wide enough to accommodate spices, tea tins and cookery jars, which can be seen at a glance. The high pull-out drawer for cereals and groceries, and the high shelf for storing large pasta pans means every inch of this unit makes a contribution.**

Space saving furniture

Think hard about the practicality of the furniture you buy, especially if space is short. Would it be a good idea to buy a bed with integral drawers underneath, for example, for storing blankets and bed linen? Some single beds come with a second bed which slides away underneath – useful for weekend guests when your bedrooms are small, or when a spare room is not an option.

A table which folds down, or chairs which stack make a lot of sense, as they can be kept tidily out of the way when not in use. The attractive box seat on page 8 has been put to wonderful use in a hallway to store collapsible garden chairs. It would be just as good for storing walking boots, Wellingtons and small garden tools.

Space saving tips and devices

18

• Under-bed trolleys make useful and accessible storage space.
• Space-saver shelves like this one and spice shelves inside cupboard doors make space work doubly hard.

• Multi-hanging hangers allow you to hang three or four times as much clothing in the same space.
• Shoe racks or stacking storage boxes, like these colourful plastic ones, work on the same principle.
• Choose mops, brushes and dustpans with loops, so they can be hung neatly out of the way when not in use.
• Use a clothes drier/airer which can be suspended from the ceiling, rather than a free standing one.
• Window seats, which can be as narrow as 60cm wide, create more seating where space is short.

Hinged lids allow them to double up as valuable storage space.
• Trunks and chests for blankets and bedding can double up as tables, especially beside a bed.
• Fit a pull-out box on castors under the first stair tread, or replace the kick-board under kitchen units with a shallow drawer for roasting trays and cake tins.
• Tools must be hung well out of a child's reach, above a workbench, possibly from a metal grid fixed to the wall (see Chapter 2: The tool room).
• Keep shelves shallow when storing bottles and jars, so that they are easier to find at a glance, and there is less risk of knocking them over.
• Before buying cupboards or having them made, make sure you have allowed for unusually shaped items: tall bottles, boots, bags and photograph albums, for example.

STORAGE CHECKLIST

• When calculating the storage space you will need, have you allowed for things you will buy in the future?

• Is there enough light? Fumbling about in a dark cupboard, loft or cellar is a waste of time, and can be dangerous.

• Is the area clean, dry and safe? Will you be able to reach safely any awkward items or those stored high up or low down (see Storage Safety)?

• When planning storage cupboards, have you left fuse boxes and electricity meters easily accessible?

• Could you use hinged or sliding doors, or even substitute curtains, where space is at a premium?

• Do you have a large cupboard or small box room which could be used just for storage, with the installation of shelves, hanging racks, etc., designed for your particular needs (see Chapter 2: The utility room).

• Can you organise items by season? There is no point in allowing thick winter clothes to take up valuable cupboard space in summer. And an ice-cream maker on a kitchen sideboard over the winter is taking up valuable space unnecessarily.

• If it is covered in dust, do you really need it?

STORAGE SAFETY

• Shelves should not be set too high or too deep for you to be able to reach them, or see what is stored there. Keep them shallow and use a small ladder or step for safety. In working areas, set shelves at your eye level where they can be reached without strain.

• The space under shelves and at the bottom of wardrobes is useful for hiding storage boxes. Put them on a trolley, or a wooden base with castors, so they can be pulled out with ease.

• Store heavy objects at waist height. If you pull heavy objects down from high shelves, or lift them up from the floor, you risk straining muscles.

• Only store on high shelves things that are quite light, such as blankets or bedding. These should be reachable at full stretch (not tip toes) or with steps or a stool.

2 What the eye doesn't see

Clutter can be very hard to live with. Most of us have been driven mad at some time by a pile of papers which needs to be dealt with, but which eventually topples under the weight of the wait. Disorganised clutter wastes time, and is frustrating. It is not particularly pretty on the eye either. The vacuum cleaner has never been central to any interior design scheme, and it takes huge flair to make piles of socks, underwear and jumpers pleasing to behold.

The majority of household items which are not decorative are best kept hidden. This isn't just aesthetics. In a small space, smooth straight lines fool the eye that the space is actually bigger. In small kitchens, bathrooms, hallways and landings, keep small details like handles and hinges simple, and make design details as unobtrusive as possible.

A cupboard is the obvious answer. Look hard at where you might be able to fit one. Cupboards can work well in unorthodox places, and doors can be cut to fit awkward angles. If the cupboard fronts are the same colour as the room itself, they will disappear into the decor. Make the doors sliding or folding and they will be even less obtrusive.

Left: **Even free standing cupboards can be simple enough to suit small spaces, yet spacious enough to serve a purpose. This attractive larder-style cupboard has pleasingly straight lines, with unfussy handles, and neat wicker baskets for storing table linen and tea towels.**
Right: **The essentials of a bathroom – bottles, brushes and towels – are hidden away inside an unusual free standing cupboard, with decorative tin panels. To give it a traditional look, the cupboard has been painted in blue/green eggshell paint, and sanded at the edges (see Chapter 4 for ideas on paint finishes for wood).**

HIDEAWAY ROOMS

Large numbers of household things are best hidden away in a place of their own, better still, in a room of their own, such as a utility room, larder or tool room.

The utility room

A utility room is perfect for storage, if you have the space (you may be able to adapt a lobby area by the back door). It keeps the practical and essential things of life in one place, where they are easy to find, and, above all, safe. These might include: washing machine, drier, freezer, vacuum cleaner, mops, buckets, sewing kit, shoe cleaning kit, clothes drier/airer, vases, tinned food, washing powders, pet food, spare kitchen rolls, boots and coats.

Safety:
• Keep clear access to fuse boxes and stop cocks.
• If the boiler is in the utility room, make sure that flammable items are kept well away from the boiler flue.
• Keep heavy and/or electrical items with flexes (irons, kitchen appliances) neatly and securely out of the way of children.
• Fix a set of hooks to the wall for hanging brushes and mops, and the ironing board, to prevent it falling.
• Make sure bleach and other poisonous cleaning fluids are kept well out of reach.

Storage:
Plastic stacking boxes, their contents clearly marked on the outside, will keep smaller items safe and easy to identify. They could be used to group items as follows.
• sewing kit
• shoe cleaning kit
• small gardening tools and gloves
• twine and Sellotape
• paint brushes, paint scrapers
• light bulbs
• starch and stain removers

Plastic baskets are useful for storing newspapers, bottles, etc., for recycling. Empty tins and cans are best kept in a bin with a lid. Hang Wellingtons out of the way on a wall-mounted boot rack.

If possible, install a sink in your utility room for dirty jobs like soaking/rinsing, or cleaning boots and brushes, which you would not want to do in the kitchen sink. A small number of kitchen units provide additional storage space, and, as they are not used as frequently as those in the kitchen, they need not be as good quality.

The larder

Before the revolutionary invention of the refrigerator, most houses had a larder or a cold room. A larder is very unusual these days, and that is our loss because there are some foods which do not enjoy the extreme cold of the refrigerator. Stored food is not particularly appealing to look at, and, with a little ingenuity, you may be able to adapt a corner by the back door, a deep kitchen cupboard, an area in the garage or, best of all, a secure, vermin-free outhouse, into the modern equivalent of the traditional larder.

• Choose a dry, cool, dark area.
• Make sure there is good ventilation, but cover any nearby windows with fly-proof gauze.
• Have plain brick or white emulsioned walls, and where possible, create cold flooring with tiles or stone (even concrete).
• Don't store food near freezers or refrigerators, which give off heat.
• Fix hooks onto timber laths, then fix the laths to the ceiling for hanging vegetables such as onions, or preserved meats.

• If possible, store food on a slate slab, held up on bricks. Slate will keep foods cool, and the space beneath is ideal for storing wine.

Foods to store in a larder:

• biscuits and sugars
• dried herbs and spices
• onions and garlic, suspended from the ceiling for all-round ventilation
• potatoes, carrots, etc., which need a dark, cool place
• cheeses, which should be wrapped and kept cool
• eggs, in wire baskets

• preserved meats, such as hams and salamis, which should be covered in gauze, and hung from the ceiling
• apples (eaters and cookers) will keep for a long time on racks where air can circulate (they should not be touching each other)
• wine, which should be kept cool and dark
• jams, chutneys and other preserves (clearly marked with date and contents), which could be stored on shelves
• tinned food

23

Above: **By adapting an otherwise blank wall, a perfect, cool environment has been created for storing jams, pickles and preserves, which can be left to mature.**

Left: **The space above your head in a larder will suit foods which need cool, dry conditions.**

The tool room, workshop or garden store

It is very important to store tools out of sight. Whilst they need to be easy to find, they can be dangerous if left where they can be tripped over, or where they are within reach of children. You might well be able to utilise the wall at the end of a garage, but failing that, garden sheds come in a range of shapes and sizes, and provide very good dry storage. Cover as much wall space as possible with wide metal mesh, so that tools can be hung up, and space is left for a workbench. Even hover mowers and strimmers, spades and rakes can be wall mounted. Small storage units for components such as screws and nails can also be wall mounted (such units are available from DIY stores). If you will be working in the tool room, it is sensible to include a large dustbin so that waste can be thrown away safely.

24

If a tool room or a garden shed is not feasible, you can buy garden storage boxes, compact, purpose-built timber constructions which will keep a certain number of garden tools safe and dry.

Safety:
- Locate a tool room as far away from the living area of the house as possible. Mess spreads!
- Make sure the flooring is solid and easy to clean.
- Install high shelves for storing garden pesticides and chemicals, especially solvents (not in a confined space, as they are flammable). Make sure the contents are marked clearly on the outside.
- Make sure sharp tools like saws and scalpels are stored with protective covers on the blades.
- Do not leave electrical items (e.g., sanders) plugged in.
- Keep fuel for mowers and strimmers in the correct storage cans.
- Install a residual current device (RCD) in case of electrical faults or accidents.
- Keep a fire extinguisher in the tool room.
- Make sure the door has a good lock, for security as well as safety.

Camouflaging clutter

There are a variety of techniques for ensuring that what the eye doesn't see, the heart won't grieve over.

Hiding a child's desk within a cupboard, for example, is a good way to shut away mess. The shelves do not need to be deep to accommodate books for homework; the stool slides and stores neatly under the desk; the message board will keep odds and ends tidied away (see Chapter 4 for how to make one yourself), and the interior has been covered in a pretty but simple wallpaper, which co-ordinates with the front of the cupboard. When the desk is not in use, the cupboard doors can be shut on homework.

Hiding away videos, CDs and tapes is also a good idea, and, although all manner of purpose-made boxes are available, a simple front opening cupboard on which the television can sit is a neat solution to the problem.

Curtains provide a simpler and less expensive camouflage than cupboards – and curtains remove the need for doors, which take up room when space is tight. These pretty yellow curtains, decorated with fun motifs, have a co-ordinating fabric backing and are attached by a fixed goblet heading (a straight, ungathered curtain requires the minimum of fabric). The shelves behind the curtain are deep enough to accommodate clothes, shoes and even toys. Instead of shelves you could store folded clothes in plastic-covered-mesh baskets, which are inexpensive and available from most large DIY stores. Children's clothes take up very little hanging space and need only a small rail at the top of the cupboard. The back wall has been covered with the same wallpaper that has been used in the room.

MAKING A DOOR CURTAIN

When the contents of a glass-fronted cupboard are far less interesting than the cupboard itself, place curtains on wooden rods inside the glass doors (the rods are held by hooks at the sides).

Method:
• You will need a piece of fabric 1½ times the total width of the glass plus 4cm for side turnings, and the same length as the glass plus 28cm for making the rod casings. You will also need wooden dowel rods slightly wider than the glass, and two small brass hooks to fix each rod.
• Turn 1cm hems down the sides of each curtain, tack and stitch.
• Fold under a double 7cm hem along the top of each curtain, and stitch close to the hem edge. Stitch again 3cm above this hem, to form a rod casing for the dowel. Repeat at the bottom edge.

• Push the dowel rods through the casings, gathering the fabric as you go, and hang the curtain by screwing the brass hooks into the inside of the doors and slipping the rods through them.

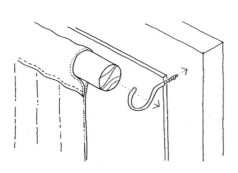

Quick and easy curtaining ideas

Curtains allow you to cheat and deceive. A uninteresting table with shelves or plenty of space beneath provides plenty of storage space when shrouded in fabric. The crisp table cloth, with contrasting corner pleats for detail, looks lovely and fresh. A cloth could be secured by a glass top, available from any reputable glass supplier who will cut it to size and smooth off the edges. A plain or cheap, free stand-ing shelving unit, filled with the little essentials of life, could also be covered in this way.

Using curtains to cover up kitchen shelving is far less expensive than cupboard doors. Apply a spray-on fabric protector because they will get very grubby over time, and, more importantly, check that the fabric is flame resistant if it is to hang close to a heat source like the cooker.

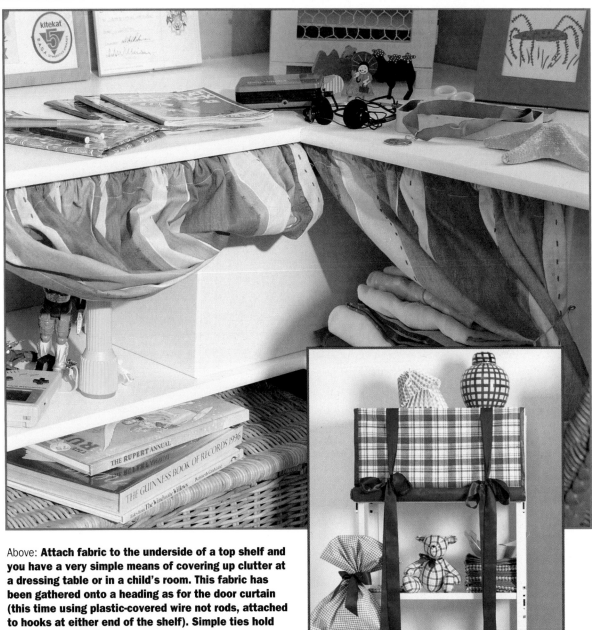

Above: **Attach fabric to the underside of a top shelf and you have a very simple means of covering up clutter at a dressing table or in a child's room. This fabric has been gathered onto a heading as for the door curtain (this time using plastic-covered wire not rods, attached to hooks at either end of the shelf). Simple ties hold the fabric back when necessary.**

Right: **These self-assembly timber shelves (from most DIY stores) have been sanded, primed and painted with two coats of gloss, then a length of cotton blue-checked fabric has been hung down the front. For added interest, the fabric has been backed with plain blue fabric, and four ties have been stitched onto the top edge of the fabric, front and back, to be secured in a pretty bow when the fabric is rolled up. Attach the curtain to the front with tacks. The contents of the shelves are packed neatly out of sight in baskets, simple draw-string laundry bags, or storage boxes covered in co-ordinating fabric (see Chapter 4 for covering boxes yourself).**

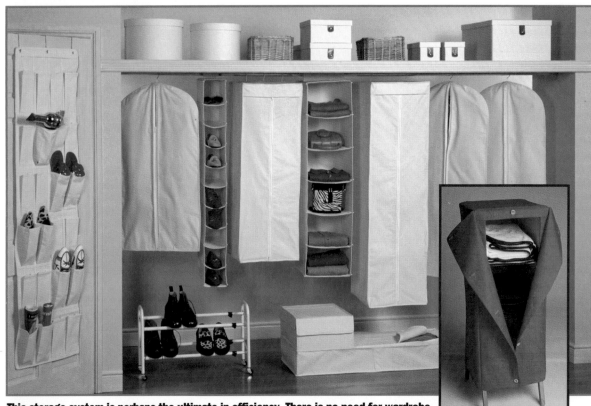

This storage system is perhaps the ultimate in efficiency. There is no need for wardrobe doors when everything is neatly zipped up or boxed away. Inset: **This ingenious Tardis wardrobe, made from cotton canvas in a variety of colours, with canvas-covered shelves, can be used to store linen, clothes and sheets permanently or temporarily. When not in use, it can be dismantled and packed away.**

Great little hideaways

• If items are hidden away, they must be easy to find. Keep sewing threads, cottons, etc., in boxes marked with a motif, perhaps one which helps you to identify the contents.

• Storage boxes need not be sophisticated or expensive. You could paint fruit boxes and use them to store socks and shoes, belts and shoe polish. They could slip easily beneath a bed, or under the bottom shelf of a wardrobe.

• CD and cassette boxes are inexpensive and easy to find, and are a very useful way to discreetly hide away a suspect taste in music!

• The old-fashioned screen **(right)** can hide a multitude of sins. Make one yourself from two or three equal-sized sheets of MDF (medium density fibreboard, available at all builders' merchants). Mark them out in curves or Gothic points, using a paper template, and cut to shape

using a jigsaw. Fix the panels together using piano hinges. Cover them with an acrylic primer/undercoat then eggshell paint and decorate the screen by stencilling a design, or cover the panels with fabric (fixed with fabric glue, leaving enough fabric to overlap the edges). Finish the edges with an interesting trim glued in place to cover the overlapping fabric. Alternatively, make two or three frames using 25mm x 25mm timber, painted or stained, and make panels with gathered or pleated fabric, tacked onto the frame.

• Keep certificates, insurance documents and important papers locked away in bankers' boxes or brightly coloured two-drawer filing cabinets from office supply shops. Less expensive ones (in less interesting colours) can be bought from second-hand office suppliers.

(For more hideaway ideas, see Chapter 4)

Small boxes, for threads and sewing kits, look pretty covered with decoupage, and finished with several layers of acrylic varnish.

3 Putting it all on show

Displaying the clutter of life, rather than hiding it away, can be the answer, especially when space is short. You may be without a loft, or lack the space for copious wardrobes. Or you may just be a squirrel by nature, unable to resist buying bits and pieces of great beauty but little practical use.

Leaving books, pictures, collections, and odds and ends out on view adds character to a room and reveals the personality of the people who live there. Colour co-ordinate or contrast your collections, and mix unusual combinations: glass and books, china figures with photographs, teapot collections with wooden boxes, the useful with the useless. Make displays interesting by varying shapes and sizes. Practical items, which might otherwise be stored away, can blend in and be less obtrusive when mixed with the purely decorative.

DISPLAY CHECKLIST

Putting it all on show is a very practical way of living. It dispenses with the need to search through cupboards, or climb loft ladders to find wayward items. Everything is accessible and easy to find, as long as you follow the golden rule: keep some kind of order.

• Be scrupulous about hygiene: items on shelves, cabinets and dressers are dust traps and create double the amount of housework.
• Don't pile shelves and dressers so high with items in everyday use that things may be knocked off while you reach for a particular jug or plate.
• Keep items you use often (books, china, glasses, bottles) at eye-level, or close at hand.
• Hang mugs, plates and utensils whenever possible to increase your storage space, and to leave work surfaces clear.

These books have been attractively displayed on natural wood shelves, making full use of the wall space, but, to break the monotony, they have been interspersed with photographs, ornaments, a clock and pictures. You might vary a run of books, too, by lying some on their side.

Living areas

Any amount can be displayed so long as it is presented in an interesting and practical way. Crystal and ornaments, for example, are fragile, so should be positioned out of reach of fiddling fingers, or where they cannot be knocked. Anything of particular value would be best kept behind glass.

The whole of life has been amassed using the modular system **(left)**, where the shelves can vary in length, and shape, and are both practical and interesting to the eye. There is a clock hung on the back wall of one of the shelves (you might choose to hang a small picture or photograph), and a desk neatly slotted into the corner. Lamps and plants add variety. The living space around the chairs and the tables is relatively clutter free, but the room reflects the character of the owners.

If you have a collection of particular interest (model cars, porcelain, antique wooden boxes, china shoes), it is worth making them the centre piece of the whole room. Choose shelving and colours for your carpets and walls, and even lighting and seating arrangements, to make the most of it (see Chapter 5).

33

The home office

The office environment can be at odds with the home, which should be a place to relax. It takes a great deal of discipline to keep the two separate, and storing items to do with work in a practical but attractive way can be hard to achieve. By their very nature, desks are messy: papers and in-trays spill and overflow. If you have a room which can be surrendered totally to the office, so much the better, but space constraints may force you to make do with a desk in the living room, so things need to be kept in order.

If your desk is on show, make sure it blends in with the rest of the house. The lighting, for example, needs to be good, but a modern anglepoise lamp will look out of place next to traditional table lamps. Look around for lighting that complements your decor – there are some beautiful reproduction desk lamps to be had. Your chair needs to be comfortable, but traditional office furniture will be at odds with most home furnishings. Try to find a chair which looks right, but which is the correct height for your desk, and helps you keep a good posture.

Keep your desk as clear as possible, so you have adequate work space. Position faxes and printers on shelves or trolleys whenever possible. Message boards can be made from corkboard, or chipboard covered in fabric or felt which co-ordinates with the rest of the room (see Chapter 4 for how to make one). For the ultimate in chic, make up a typewriter or computer cover in the fabric used for the blind or curtains. There's no need to be a slave to tradition!

Office equipment companies have come on in leaps and bounds in terms of producing attractive filing cabinets, files, and boxes, in bold colours and patterns. Your workplace can now look less formal, and you can colour co-ordinate the boxes to identify their contents. Don't forget to include pots for pencils and pens.

Build shelves surrounding a desk (which could be created out of a wider shelf) so that books and papers are stored neatly but are close to hand when you need them. Put them on adjustable brackets (see Chapter 5) and they can be spaced to fit files, phonebooks, computer disk boxes and stationery exactly. These shelves blend in well because they have been painted the same colour as the walls and radiator.

The greatest friend of the cook is the humble little hook. It keeps things close to hand, like these mugs which add a fun dimension to the zigzag pelmet in this small kitchen. Butchers hooks, available from good kitchen suppliers, can also suspend cooking ingredients, like garlic, onions or dried herbs.

Kitchens

In the kitchen, order and hygiene are the priorities. The kitchen is a working area, and, whilst it is satisfying to have a system which is pleasing to the eye, you also must be able to find and reach everything with the greatest ease, and minimum effort. The need for hygiene goes without saying. Kitchens often accumulate and create large amounts of dirt and rubbish, so they must be easy to clean.

Frequently used items like colanders and other utensils could be hung from wooden or stainless steel rails on butchers' hooks, out of the way but near enough to reach. Bottles and cooking ingredients are best kept at eye level, and storable items tucked away in cupboards or drawers underneath, leaving the cook with a work surface clear for food preparation. You could keep drawer fronts open and use pull-out baskets instead.

Keeping crockery on display cuts down the chances of chipping or breakage. This was the whole reason behind wooden plate racks and the below-stairs pine dresser of days gone by. The dresser has now found its way in to common usage everywhere, but you don't need to go the whole hog. If you lack the room for a whole dresser, shallow dresser-top shelving for displaying a dinner service will do the trick.

In this kitchen, where there would be no room for a large dresser base, shallow dresser-top style shelving has been used for a pretty collection of dinner plates. Such shelves should always have a bar, and/or lip on the shelf to stop plates slipping.

Kitchen units need not be custom made to provide good storage. A mixture of styles with free standing furniture can look very original. A browse around antique or junk shops might turn up a table like this one, with its useful shelf underneath. It has been scrubbed and limed, and teamed up with a custom-made unit which has shallow shelves and a practical plate rack.

Where cooking ingredients and utensils are left on display, keep them as attractive to look at as possible.

• Glass jars, especially six or seven in the same style, look very appealing filled with interesting colours and shapes such as pasta, coloured pulses, preserves, or fruit. They are relatively inexpensive too. Try asking your local confectionery shop for a supplier of the large sweet jars used by retailers, or use kilner jars.

• Glass bottles look just as good. There is a wide choice of bottles containing intriguing oils and vinegars.

• It's well worth keeping your eye out for old tins or Oxo boxes, though some are rare and fetch quite a price.

• Less interesting contents, such as flour and sugar, can be concealed by painting glass jars, a technique used to great effect on these chain-store glass-stoppered jars. Use an oil-based paint (gloss, eggshell or enamel), thinning the first layer with white spirit. Any paint used on glass is inclined to chip easily, though this is no problem if the jars are not in everyday use.

• Keeping pans and utensils in the same style and colour will help prevent a jumbled look. Stainless steel, with its high-tech look, is ideal because it is so easy to keep clean.

Linen and blankets

There is something very attractive about a pile of linen, or beautifully coloured towels, blankets and quilts piled neatly in a cupboard or on a shelf.

If you plan to display bedding, quantity is all! Pile it high, keeping contrasting colours together, sheets and pillowcases crisp and well ironed, towels and blankets neatly folded with the rounded side outwards. Towels look excellent on a bathroom shelf, in colours which match curtains or paintwork, and placed next to interesting bottles full of jewel-coloured bubble bath or bath oil.

4 Practical and pretty

The need for storage is a marvellous excuse to seek out interesting and pretty bits of furniture. Once you have worked out what needs a home, there is no end to the pots, boxes, cabinets, boards, shelving systems, cupboards or wardrobes your possessions can be stored in or displayed on.

Made-to-measure furniture

Custom-built fitted furniture certainly has its place, and investing in expertly made bespoke units, clever storage systems or traditional chests of drawers or cupboards makes sense. Good carpentry unfortunately comes at a price, so, if you are thinking of fitted furniture, ask yourself if the investment is worthwhile. Would it be better, where possible, to have free standing bookcases bolted to the wall, so you can take them with you when you move house?

If you decide to employ a craftsman, the following guide-lines should help to avoid problems and disappointment.
• Get two or three estimates for the work.
• See work that your chosen carpenter has done for other people before confirming the job. Nothing beats recommendation.
• Make sure you know exactly what materials will be used, especially inside cupboards. Using timber throughout, rather than laminated chipboard, is more expensive, but much more attractive.
• Make your own drawings, or find a picture in a book or magazine, and discuss in detail the various finishes required (beading, handles, hinges, etc.).
• Even on the smallest job mistakes can happen, or there can be misunderstandings about design, so try if possible to be there when the job commences, until you are happy with the way it is going.
• Unless you are having something huge built, it is not usual for a contractor to supply an invoice until the job is completed. Make sure you are entirely happy before you pay.

Opposite: **This dresser has been painted to fit in with its crisp white surroundings, and the blue gingham curtains, table cloth and fabric wall covering make a stunning show with the checked crockery.**
Left: **Made-to-measure furniture can be a very efficient use of space because, as this book case shows, it will be made to fit your particular requirements exactly.**

Dull furniture can be transformed with a little inspiration: this very ordinary new pine wardrobe unit has been jazzed up with pack-of-card stencils.

Adapting ready-made furniture

A browse around antique shops or markets, even budget chain stores, will turn up all manner of unusual and sometimes beautiful pieces of furniture which could fit your needs.

Furniture designers for the high-street shops now produce attractive ready-made furniture, even at the lower end of the price range, so it's always worth looking around for what you might be able to transform.

New pine, much cheaper than old, lends itself well to painting or staining and, as its colour is not as warm as old pine, can look much better for it (see box on page 44 for ideas with wood).

It is also possible to buy 'blank' furniture (including storage chests and boxes) which is untreated, ready for you to let loose your imagination and decorate as you like. The satisfying part is that such pieces are unique and make your home just a little more individual.

Above left: **A little extravagance may be worthwhile: an oak corner cupboard, though expensive, will display and store everyday china in the best possible way.**

Above right: **Spice drawers, like these cherry wood ones, make a brilliant storage solution, though you may well have trouble remembering what you put in which drawer!**

Below: **Very simple MDF (medium density fibreboard) shelving and cupboards in this child's room have been brightened up with bold eggshell paint in vibrant colours. The shelf over the radiator and shaped shelving on the wardrobe end help to make brilliant use of space, for comparatively little money.**

An ordinary chest or cupboard from a junk shop, an indifferent modern piece from a budget furniture store, or blank untreated furniture can become magical with the use of paint or stain, and a little inspiration. The effort of doing the job properly is well worthwhile as it gives a durable finish.

Painting

Make sure all surfaces are clean, dry and dust free before you start. Furniture cleaner, applied with a rag, will remove any previous layers of wax.

All raw wood needs primer and undercoat to cut down on absorption, and to provide a base for the top coat. An oil-based primer (to seal against moisture) is advisable if the wood will be in wet or steamy conditions. Combined acrylic primer/undercoats save time, are more manageable and dry quickly. If you have a large surface to cover, flat oil paint, for trade use (minimum 5 litre cans), will do the job very efficiently. Wood which has dark knotting (especially pine) will need to be treated with knotting fluid, to stop the knots showing through the top coat. MDF (medium density fibreboard) has the advantage of a smooth surface with no knotting.

The most common types of top coat are eggshell, vinyl matt or gloss. Gloss is harder to apply, but leaves a smooth, hard wearing finish. Eggshell/lustre paints give a more matt finish to woodwork; select one with added polyurethane which will better withstand knocks. Microporous paints are most suitable for wood, as they allow it to breathe, and leave a sheen finish. They are particularly suitable for outdoor use (no undercoat is necessary).

Staining

Staining can change the colour dramatically or subtly, depending on how bold you are feeling. Buy pre-mixed, water- or spirit-based stains or dyes, and apply with a brush or cloth. Remember that stains soak into the grain, so the colour can't be changed if you change your mind. Test the colour on the invisible underside of the piece of furniture first. After applying stain, sand the wood lightly, and apply a second coat if necessary. Finish with a non-yellowing acrylic varnish, sanded down lightly between coats to ensure good adhesion and to remove any specks of dust. Stains mixed with polyurethane sealers can be removed with chemicals if the colour is wrong, or you want to change it. MDF does not look good stained or waxed.

Waxing

Waxes are a less dramatic but very effective means of colouring wood. They come in a variety of natural colours. Apply with a rag.

Clever storage ideas

As fast as we acquire bits and pieces these days, companies come up with brilliant ideas for storing them. Their ideas may not always be the cheapest way to solve your storage problems, but it is often worth paying for someone else's ingenuity!

When you need storage ideas, look away from conventional solutions and you might find the answer. High-tech industrial shelving, for example, would be ideal in a garage or tool shed, but also very attractive in a kitchen, displaying chrome pans and utensils.

This plastic hanging unit solves the problem when shelf space is short. There are hanging shoe tidies which work on the same principle, keeping six or seven pairs of shoes in canvas compartments.

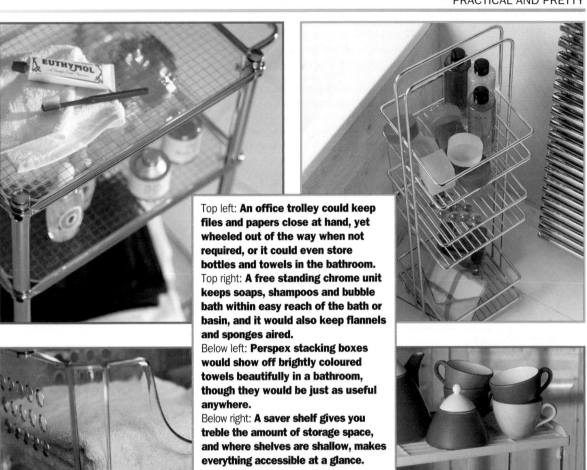

Top left: **An office trolley could keep files and papers close at hand, yet wheeled out of the way when not required, or it could even store bottles and towels in the bathroom.**
Top right: **A free standing chrome unit keeps soaps, shampoos and bubble bath within easy reach of the bath or basin, and it would also keep flannels and sponges aired.**
Below left: **Perspex stacking boxes would show off brightly coloured towels beautifully in a bathroom, though they would be just as useful anywhere.**
Below right: **A saver shelf gives you treble the amount of storage space, and where shelves are shallow, makes everything accessible at a glance.**

Left: **A honeycomb unit is ideal in a bedroom drawer for tidying away ties, socks or underwear.**
Right: **These collapsible plastic boxes would be especially useful in a utility room, storeroom or garage.**

Making it yourself

Creating your own storage systems, or adding a personal touch with a coat of paint or length of fabric, will result in a storage style which is original and costs little.

These drawers have been primed and undercoated, covered in a base coat, then painted free-hand with simple pictures. Draw your designs freehand in pencil first, using a template to keep the size of each picture consistent. Measure carefully so the designs appear in the same place each time. Make a checked pattern with strips of masking tape and paint the squares in between. Finish the chest in two or three thin coats of acrylic varnish to resist chipping. The terracotta plant pots for storing pencils are a splendid finishing touch. They have been covered in two or three layers of vinyl matt paint (as terracotta is very absorbent) and finished with an acrylic, non-yellowing varnish.

Cardboard storage boxes have been painted in co-ordinating and alternate colours (finished with an acrylic varnish to stop chipping), to make this shelving unit totally unique. The result is practical, easy on the eye, and keeps mess tucked away in a neat and streamlined way.

INEXPENSIVE STORAGE CONTAINERS

• Keep tights in a string shopping bag hung on the inside of a wardrobe.
• Keep invitations or bills to pay on a simple message board (see page 48 for how to make one).
• Store toys in bright plastic stacker boxes, or inexpensive wicker laundry baskets.

• Cover sturdy cardboard boxes with fabric (see page 28) and use for storage on utility room shelves, or above cupboards. Shoe boxes could store tapes or CDs.
• Baskets come in a vast range of shapes and sizes, and are very reasonably priced. Use baskets with or without handles to store magazines, mail-order catalogues, useful notes and papers.
• Keep spare lavatory rolls in inexpensive round baskets near to the toilet.
• Store pants or socks rolled into pairs in matching shallow baskets, which can then sit prettily on an open shelf.

Hat boxes sit easily on shelves or on top of wardrobes and they can be made very attractive when covered with fabric which matches the overall room style. To cover them you will need:

- main fabric
- hat box
- fabric glue
- roller blind stiffener, if necessary
- tape
- cord, if required

Measuring up:

You will need a rectangle of fabric to cover the sides of the box, and a narrower rectangle to cover the sides of the lid, the lengths of which will be the circumference of the box. The width needed for the sides of the box will be the height of the box, adding 5cm for finishing at the bottom edge. The width needed for the sides of the lid will be the height of the lid, plus 5cm top and bottom for finishing off. For the top of the lid, place the lid on the fabric, draw around it and cut out a circle of fabric, to come just inside the lid's edge.

Making up:

1. Apply stiffener, if you choose to use it, to the edges of all fabric that will show on the box, and allow to dry.
2. Stick the long rectangle of fabric around the sides of the box, aligning one edge with the top edge of the box.
3. Snip into the overlapping fabric along the bottom edge at regular intervals. Spread glue 5cm in along the base of the box and fold snipped edge onto glue, square by square.

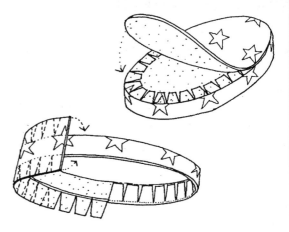

4. Stick the narrower rectangle on to the sides of the lid, leaving a 5cm overlap at the top and bottom. Snip the overlap at regular intervals as before and spread glue under the rim of the lid. Fold the overlap over and stick it under the rim of the lid. Repeat for the top of the lid.
5. Stick the fabric circle on the top of the lid, covering the snipped overlap. Leave until glue has dried thoroughly.

Note: You can add a cord or ribbon handle simply by punching holes at opposite sides of the box, and threading your cord or ribbon through, knotting the ends on the inside.

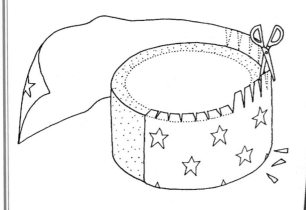

For a simple but effective board for notes and reminders, you will need:

• piece of chipboard cut to required size and shape
• piece of fabric or felt to cover the chipboard, the size of the board plus 10cm on all sides for overlap (possibly matching or contrasting with fabric already in the room)
• piece of felt, 1cm smaller all round than the board
• small tacks and a small hammer
• enough co-ordinating bias binding or tape to criss-cross over the board, including 5cm overlap at each end
• fabric glue
• paper fasteners (optional)

1. Making sure the board is dust free, spread glue thinly over one side. Lay the fabric, right side up, on top of the glued board and smooth it out to make sure there are no creases.
2. Carefully turn the board over, and snip off the corners of the fabric. Spread glue around the edge of the reverse side of the board and stick down the overlapping fabric.

3. Cut lengths of bias binding or tape, to cross the board diagonally at regular intervals. The more diagonals there are, the more places you will have to tuck notes and reminders.

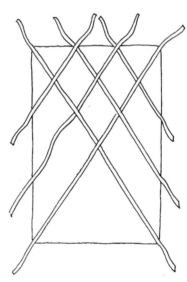

4. Turn the board to the reverse side and tack the binding or tape to the back lightly with a small hammer, making sure the tape is not twisted. Make the tape taught, but slack enough for you to slip messages and notes beneath it.

5. Spread glue around the edges of the rectangle of felt, and place it over the reverse side of the board, covering the snipped edges of fabric, and the ends of tape.

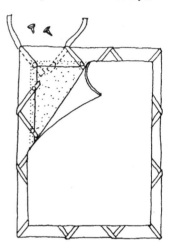

Note: a nice finishing touch is to punch a small hole where two pieces of tape cross, and to fasten them together with gold paper fasteners.
• Cover cork board with felt or fabric as above to make a simple pin-board.
• Use an old decorative picture frame to make a border for your message board.

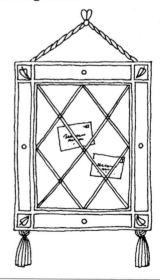

48

The pockets can be made to suit whatever it is you wish to store. You will need:

• two rectangles of strong fabric (e.g., calico) to size required, plus 5cm on the length and 1cm on the width
• contrasting fabric for the pockets
• two pieces of wooden dowel, cut to the finished width less 2 cm
• eyelet tool and eyelets

1. Place two rectangles of suitably strong fabric right sides together (calico would be good for heavier items), and stitch along the longest two sides, 0.5cm from the edge. Turn right sides out and press. Turn over both edges together 0.5cm at the top and again 2cm to create a casing, and stitch. Repeat at the bottom. Slide pieces of dowel into the casings and secure at each end. Press in an eyelet at each end

2. For the pockets, cut out squares or rectangles of contrasting (and suitably strong) fabric to the sizes required, plus 1cm turnover on three sides, and 2cm on the top. Turn over the edges of the pockets, 1cm on three sides, 1cm twice along the top edge, and press. Hem the top.

3. Place the pockets on the backing fabric and pin, tack and stitch in place, remembering to leave the tops open. Choose an attractive hemming stitch for detail.

4. Hang with cord looped through eyelets.

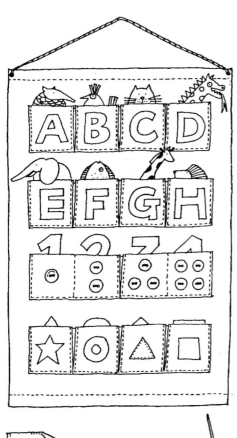

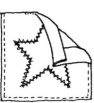

5 Shelving

No home should be without an abundance of shelves. They are, after all, the ultimate display and storage system. Everything is there at a glance, they can be built to your most detailed specification, and, with a bit of imagination, can be made to look elegant, appealing, and even witty.

Good shelving can become the centre piece of a room – think carefully about a type of shelving which will complement or contrast with your style, and about how best to display your collections, books and ornaments on the shelves. Should they be plain so as not to overpower a bright collection of Art Deco jugs? Would heavy tomes benefit from quirky shelving decorations or unusual brackets? Would a pink colour wash on the walls of an alcove complement a collection of pink floral porcelain? Step beyond traditional ideas on shelving to put your own signature on your particular system.

TYPES OF SHELVING

Free standing

These are of course the easiest to install. The benefit is that you can move them around a room as the mood takes you; they come in a mixture of materials (wood, chrome and wood, plastic, steel, aluminium) and when you move house, you take them with you. The downside is that they are not always as strong as built-in or supported shelving, and you are at the mercy of the designer for style and size. When you buy old shelves from an antique shop, what you gain on charm, you may lose in practical usefulness.

Non-adjustable shelves

Of the supported shelving systems, these are the easiest to put up, whether in an alcove or along a wall. They can be to whatever length, width or shape is required, and you can add interesting brackets for detail (see page 59 for ideas). The downside is the fact that they are non-adjustable.

Adjustable shelves and modular units

These give much more room for manoeuvre, and even ready-made, shop-bought shelving systems should offer a good variety of options on shape and shelf height. Unfortunately, you are more than likely to be able to see the support system, which is not always very attractive.

DIFFERENT SHELVING MATERIALS

So long as it is able to support what you choose to put on it, virtually anything can be used for shelving. The price will vary, of course, as will the finished effect.

Timber

There are many options available in hardwood, and the better quality the timber (oak, ash, beech or mahogany) the better it will look in its natural state. The disadvantage with timber is that it is very expensive, and does not always come from renewable sources. A softwood like pine (especially that used for window sills) is cheaper, and can look very effective, especially when stained. Chipboard (particle board), unless it has a melamine or timber veneer, and plywood both need to be painted to look good enough to display items on, especially if they are in direct light.

Timber is a very workable material, and, as with these kitchen shelves, can be cut and fitted exactly as desired.

MDF (medium density fibreboard) is an excellent choice because it has a smooth surface, without knots, which lends itself to being painted in interesting colours. It will also not warp if the shelf is above a radiator.

Metal

Metal shelves are commonly used in shop displays or industrial situations, because they are so strong and hard wearing. These qualities might also make them appropriate in the home. Metal is also easy to keep clean, and will work well with a high-tech interior, though don't be a slave to consistency: modern metal shelving could look very good next to traditional timber fittings, especially in a kitchen or bathroom. Metal is particularly good in the steamy conditions of a bathroom, where unseasoned timber can warp. Contact commercial or industrial suppliers for units.

Glass and acrylic

This is perhaps the most interesting shelving material, from a style point of view, though not necessarily from a practical one. Glass is the better looking of the two options (it doesn't scratch like acrylic) but it is also the heaviest and the most fragile. You will need special brackets for glass, and the glass itself should come from a specialist supplier, who will cut it for you, and smooth the edges. However, the advantages of glass may outweigh all these considerations. It can be etched for detail, and glass shelving is particularly attractive across a window, where it will show off glass and crystal displays beautifully without blocking out light. It is also an excellent way of disguising an unattractive view!

Load bearing guidelines

The choice of materials and supports depends entirely on what is to be stored on the shelves. It would be unnecessary to install sturdy shelving for a collection of china or glass ornaments, whereas glass would be inadvisable for a run of books (ten hardbacks weigh at least 40kg).

Material	Thickness	Max span
MDF (medium density fibreboard)	12mm	45cm
	19mm	80cm
	25mm	100cm
Faced chipboard	15mm	50cm
	19mm	60cm
	25mm	75cm
Plywood	12mm	45cm
	19mm	80cm
	25mm	100cm
Timber	15mm	50cm
	22mm	70cm
	28mm	106cm
Glass		Available in 4mm, 6mm, 8mm, 10mm thicknesses. Glass weighs a great deal, so the shelf span must be worked out in conjunction with the weight of the load. Ask your supplier for advice. More than 50-60cm would not be advisable.

Wall fixings

Shelving will only be as strong as the fixings you use. Most shelving systems are supported by wood screws inserted into plugs (rawl plugs), and the length and gauge of screw is determined by the weight to be supported. For most shelves, 50-75mm screws will suffice, but you must have at least 25mm of screw beyond the support into a solid wall, plus the thickness of the plaster. In hollow walls, wood screws do not have an adequate grip, and a cavity-wall fixing device will be necessary (a collapsible anchor or spring toggle).

The ribs on a heavy-duty plug give greater pull-out resistance and are for use in brick, high-density blocks and concrete. For lighter loads use a general purpose plug.
Shelving which will be supporting a very heavy load will need a masonry bolt (expansion anchor).
A plasterboard plug spreads the load behind the board. The heavier the load, the more heavy-duty should be the plug, the strongest being the gravity toggle.

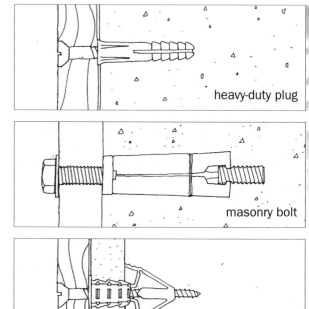

heavy-duty plug

masonry bolt

plasterboard plug

Shelving supports: some ideas

Ready-made shelving comes with a variety of clever bracket systems, including support clips, which slot into the side of the shelving system, or self-support studs which work in much the same way. The following ideas are more suitable for shelves which you make yourself.

Open wall shelving

The shelves can be adjusted by moving the steel support brackets into different slots on the upright.

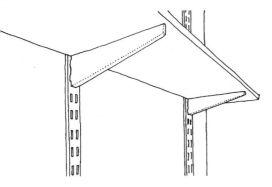

A simple timber gallows bracket: the cross piece is set into notches on the other two pieces.

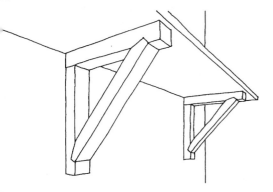

Fixed steel shelf brackets can be bought in most hardware stores. They come in a variety of sizes and even colours, and they are very strong. Look out too for aluminium cantilevered brackets.

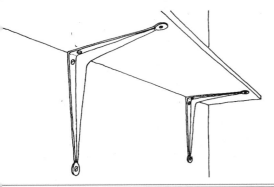

Alcove shelving

A timber support, on which the shelf (even glass) can rest, provides the simplest system of all. Once painted in the same colour as the wall or shelves themselves, such supports are also the least obvious.

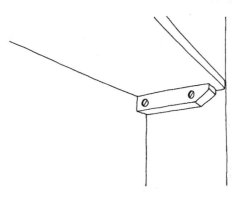

A timber shelf grooved at each end, and slid over screws with sawn-off heads looks neat but is only suitable for light displays.

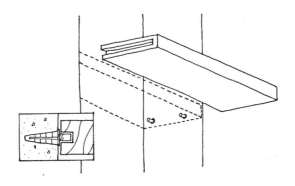

Giving shelving a magic touch

Even the dullest shelves can be transformed by decorative edging or interesting brackets.

The edge on these white shelves has been cut from MDF. The process involves the dextrous use of a jigsaw but the result is very effective. Alternatively, the cheat's way is to buy strips of ready-cut edging which stick to the shelf edge.

Right: **These woven-willow shelves are simplicity itself, show off small towels and linen very effectively, and could be made up by any capable basket weaver. They are supported with simple wooden strips on either wall (for tips on fixing alcove shelving see box on page 59).**

Bottom right: **Lacquered copper shelves on a mild-steel frame are an original option, which would look good in a kitchen. A very clinical look is avoided by including a wavy decorative edge. A blacksmith would be able to produce your own design (this is best kept simple).**

Below: **Plaster leaves, stuck on with a glue gun, are a witty and inexpensive touch, and though they could be painted, are most effective here in white. For a change, the items on the shelf complement the shelves, not vice versa.**

On a budget

A plain timber-board wall hanging can be transformed by gluing short pieces of interesting fringing to the front. With the very small amount you would need, you could afford to use very good-quality fringing.

Above: **More decorative than practical, a moulded plaster bracket acts as a shelf in itself. Original plaster mouldings are expensive and hard to find, but there are plenty of reproduction ones, often fashioned in whimsical Cupid figures. Kitsch but quite fun!**

Top right: **Adding a decorative touch need not be expensive. Thick cartridge paper cut into an interesting pattern, with the addition of simple motifs, is very effective. Quality wrapping paper or wallpaper would do just as well.**

Right: **Fabric, like paper, is an extremely economical way to brighten up shelf edges. Here the fabric has been stuck to the shelf with fabric glue, and an edging piece has been hemmed top and bottom, stiffened with fabric stiffener, gathered and tacked discreetly onto the edge of the shelf. Calculate your edging strip to be 2½ times the length of the shelf itself. It is also advisable to use a fabric protector.**

Other ideas

• Decoupage shelves: cut-out motifs stuck onto painted and prepared shelves, and covered in layers of acrylic, non-yellowing varnish.

• Shaped shelving: particularly effective in an alcove. Use a cardboard template on timber or MDF and cut using a jigsaw.

• Alternate colours: for a very colourful decor for a child's room, paint each shelf a different or alternate colour, and contrast the brackets too.

• Wire mesh: high tech and very practical, especially in kitchens or bathrooms.

• Etched glass: look out for interesting window panes which might be adapted, once cut and smoothed at the edges by a professional glass cutter (see page 59 for advice on the type of supports needed).

• Let your imagination go wild and create your own shaped brackets out of MDF, using a template and making deft use of a jigsaw.

Acknowledgements

There are a great number of shops and businesses which supply furniture and accessories invaluable to those looking for storage solutions. We would like to thank the following companies for supplying photographs of their products for use in this book:

Habitat (Tel: 01645 334433) for open shelving on page 51.

The Holding Company (Tel: 0171-610-9160) for storage accessories on pages 28.

Lakeland Plastics (Tel: 01539 488100) for storage accessories on pages 18, 44 and 45.

Lido Mail Order (Tel: 01702 77928) for the Tardis wardrobe on page 28.

MACMILLAN

First published in 1997 by Boxtree
an imprint of Macmillan Publishers Ltd
25 Eccleston Place, London SW1W 9NF
and Basingstoke
Associated companies throughout the world

ISBN 0 7522 1116 1

9 8 7 6 5 4 3 2 1

A CIP catalogue entry for this book is available from the British Library.

Front cover photographs by: main picture, Christopher Drake; left inset, James Merrell; right inset, S. Brown, reproduced courtesy of *Homes & Ideas* magazine and Robert Harding Syndication

Designed by Robert Updegraff
Illustrations by Julia Glynn-Smith
Printed and bound in Italy by Manfrini

Shelving and Storage is one of a series of books published in association with *Homes & Ideas* magazine. Also available are: *Children's Rooms*, *Window Dressing* and *Floors and Flooring*. All the books in the series are available from bookshops, recommended retail price £4.99, or you can order direct from the publisher: Boxtree, an imprint of Macmillan General Books C. S., Book Service by Post, PO Box 29, Douglas I-O-M, IM99 1BQ; tel: 01624 675137; fax: 01624 670923; Internet: http/www.book-post.co.uk. There is a charge of 75 pence per book for postage and packing. Overseas customers please allow £1.00 per copy for post and packing.

Homes & Ideas is published monthly by Southbank Publishing Group, IPC Magazines Ltd, King's Reach Tower, Stamford Street, London SE1 9LS. For subscription enquiries and overseas orders call 01444–445555 (fax no: 01444–445599). Please send orders, address changes and all correspondence to: IPC Magazines Ltd, Oakfield House, 35 Perrymount Road, Haywards Heath, West Sussex RH16 3DH. All cheques should be made payable to IPC Magazines Ltd. Alternatively, you can call the subscription credit card hotline (UK orders only) on 01622–778778.